Extreme In-line Skating

John Crossingham & Bobbie Kalman

Crabtree Publishing Company

www.crabtreebooks.com

Created by Bobbie Kalman

Dedicated by Heather Fitzpatrick
To Bert and Sandy Diehl, newlyweds at last

Editor-in-chief
Bobbie Kalman

Writing team
John Crossingham
Bobbie Kalman

Substantive editor
Niki Walker

Project editor
Kelley MacAulay

Editors
Amanda Bishop
Kathryn Smithyman
Molly Aloian

Art director
Robert MacGregor

Computer design
Katherine Kantor

Production coordinator
Heather Fitzpatrick

Photo research
Kelley MacAulay
Laura Hysert

Consultant
Kalinda Mathis, Executive Director
International Inline Skating Association

Photographers
AP/Wide World Photos: pages 6, 19, 21, 22, 25 (bottom), 27
Patrick Batchelder: pages 9 (top), 15, 16, 18, 23, 29
Bruce Curtis: pages 9 (bottom), 14, 17 (bottom)
First Light: pages 7, 25 (top), 26
Manna Photography by Judy Manna: pages 8, 17 (top)
Painet Stock Photos: Harry Meister: page 30; Stew Milne: page 20
All other images by Corbis Images and PhotoDisc

Illustrations
Robert MacGregor: pages 10-11, 24
Margaret Amy Reiach: page 13
Bonna Rouse: page 28

Crabtree Publishing Company

www.crabtreebooks.com   1-800-387-7650

PMB 16A	612 Welland Avenue	73 Lime Walk
350 Fifth Avenue	St. Catharines	Headington
Suite 3308	Ontario	Oxford
New York, NY	Canada	OX3 7AD
10118	L2M 5V6	United Kingdom

Cataloging-in-Publication Data
Crossingham, John.
  Extreme in-line skating / John Crossingham & Bobbie Kalman.
    p. cm. -- (Extreme sports no limits series)
Includes an index.
Contents: Keep it in-line--From the ice to the street--The next waves--Skating styles--Meet the board--Skateparks--The fundamentals--Grind it, slide it--Grab it, flip it--Face off--Legends of the sport--The new generation--Take it in stride--Safe keeping.
  ISBN 0-7787-1667-8 (RLB) -- ISBN 0-7787-1713-5 (pbk.)
  1. In-line skating--Juvenile literature. 2. Extreme sports--Juvenile literature. [1. In-line skating. 2. Extreme sports.] I. Kalman, Bobbie. II. Title. III. Series.
  GV859.73.C75 2003
  796.21--dc22
                                                              2003016192
                                                              LC

CONTENTS

KEEP IT IN-LINE

Some of the fastest-growing **individual sports** in the world involve in-line skating. In an individual sport, athletes perform alone. The two main types of competitive in-line skating are **aggressive in-line** and **speed skating**. Aggressive in-line is based on daring **tricks**, or moves. Speed skating features high-speed races. This book focuses mainly on aggressive in-line, the most popular type of competitive in-line skating in North America. You can read more about speed skating on pages 24-27.

MORE THAN A SPORT

Aggressive in-line has its own **culture**. A culture is a set of values that a group of people shares. Skating culture includes its own music, clothing, and way of talking. Hip-hop and punk rock are a big part of the scene. Companies including England Clothing and Mind Game design popular clothing for in-line skaters. There are even video games that allow players to skate as their favorite **professionals** or "pros."

TO THE EXTREME

For a lot of people, in-line skating is a fun way to get around, spend free time, or get in shape. Aggressive in-line is more than just a casual activity, however. It's an **extreme sport**. Extreme sports are fast-paced and difficult, and they can be dangerous. The best extreme skaters are often pros—skating is their job. They constantly push themselves to create and perform tough new tricks. It takes years of serious training to become a pro skater.

USE EXTREME CAUTION

You may be inspired to try some of the moves you see in this book. Before you strap on your skates, remember that the athletes shown here are professionals. They are skilled enough to handle tricks that are much too dangerous for other skaters to try. Their moves are meant to be admired—not copied!

5

FROM RINK TO STREET

The history of in-line skating actually begins with the roller skate, which was invented in 1761. Early roller skates were quite basic—they only moved straight ahead. In 1863, James Plimpton made the first roller skates that turned. In the late 1800s, other inventions such as **bearings** and **toe brakes** made it even easier to turn and stop roller skates. Roller skating became safer and more fun. By the 1950s, it was popular across America. Restaurants even featured waitresses on roller skates!

Early roller skates were sandals with two pairs of metal or wooden wheels on the bottom of each one. In the 1960s, **polyurethane**, or plastic, wheels were introduced. These safer, smoother wheels allowed skaters to perform fancier moves than ever before. In the 1970s, **roller rinks** mixed disco music and skating. Enthusiasm for roller skating exploded. By the end of the '70s, however, disco's popularity faded, and so did that of roller skating.

BLADING BEGINS

In 1980, Scott and Brennan Olson invented in-line skates that, unlike roller skates, looked and felt like hockey skates. The brothers wanted a way to practice hockey in the summer. Within a few years, their skates, called Rollerblades, became a huge success. Other companies soon began making in-line skates, and more and more people gave in-line skating a try.

GETTING AGGRESSIVE

In the early 1990s, some in-line skaters began trying extreme skateboarding, BMX, and surfing tricks on their skates. These skaters became the first aggressive in-line skaters. They then invented tricks that were impossible to perform on skateboards. Companies such as Salomon, Roces, and K2 designed skates just for aggressive riding. The **Aggressive Skating Association (ASA)** was formed in 1995 to help promote the new sport. In the late '90s, aggressive in-line became known around the world.

TIMELINE:

1761: roller skates are invented by Joseph Merlin
1819: Monsieur Petitbled invents the first skates with wheels set in a row
1863: roller skates that turn are invented by James Plimpton
1866: Plimpton builds the first roller rink
1876: toe brakes are created, making it easier to stop
1884: bearings are added to roller-skate wheels, making them roll more smoothly
1937: **Roller Skating Association (RSA)** is formed
1979: roller skating's popularity fades
1981: first in-line races are held
1982: first year of Athens-to-Atlanta in-line race
1988: more than a million pairs of Rollerblades sold in the U.S.
1991: **International Inline Skating Association (IISA)** is formed
1992: Roller hockey is played as an exhibition sport at the Barcelona Olympics
1993: Chris Edwards becomes first pro aggressive in-line skater
1995: the first **X Games** are held

Old-fashioned roller skates

7

DIFFERENT STROKES

Aggressive in-line borrows many of its tricks and much of its style from other extreme sports. Aggressive in-line's two main styles are **vert** and **street**. Most skaters prefer one style to the other.

STRAIGHT UP

Vert skating is all about "getting air." Skaters ride up and down large ramps to build up speed and launch themselves high into the air. In fact, vert is short for "**vertical**," which means "straight up and down." While in midair, skaters perform tricks known as **aerials**. They have to get air to do these high-flying moves. Skaters also perform balancing and sliding tricks on the edges of ramps.

*A vert ramp is called a **pipe ramp** because it looks like the bottom half of a giant pipe.*

8

HIT THE PAVEMENT

Street in-line started in cities such as Los Angeles and New York. Skaters began finding ways to use railings, stairs, benches, and other objects in their surroundings as skating **obstacles**. An obstacle is something a skater uses to perform tricks. Street tricks include anything from leaping and flipping over a giant flight of stairs to **grinding**, or sliding on the frame of the skates, along a curb or railing.

Street is the most popular style of in-line skating.

Performing tricks in a fakie stance adds an extra challenge.

FRONT TO BACK

No matter which style they skate, all aggressive skaters use the same terms to describe their body positions during tricks. Here is some basic in-line body talk:

Frontside: describes a trick performed with the skater's chest facing the obstacle
Backside: describes a trick performed with the skater's back facing the obstacle
Fakie: describes a trick done while moving backward
Switch stance: a change in the direction of a skater's body position during a grind trick

Aggressive in-line skates are made to be fast, durable, and comfortable. The foot is placed inside a boot. Some boots have a hard plastic shell, whereas others are made of strong padded fabrics. The liner inside the boot is soft and cushioned for comfort. Most skates are tightened with a combination of laces and plastic straps called **fastenings**. Aggressive in-line skates, shown right, usually have four wheels, which are attached to a long **frame**.

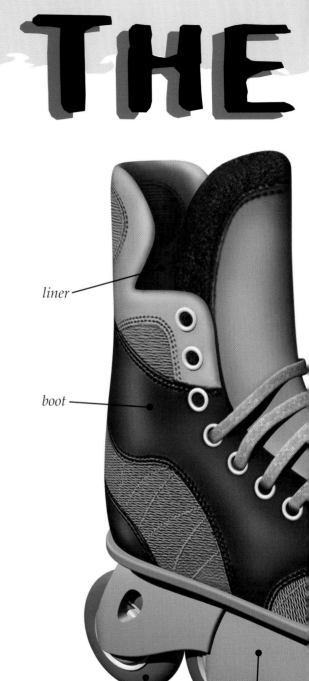

liner

boot

wheels

frame

AGGRESSIVE WHEELS

Aggressive skate wheels each have an outside edge and an inside edge. Skaters lean on the edges when turning or performing grinds. In-line wheels are made of a plastic called polyurethane, which makes them fast, smooth, and able to grip the ground well. Aggressive skate wheels are slightly smaller than **recreational** skate wheels.

SKATES

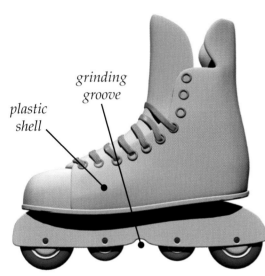

plastic shell

grinding groove

laces

*Aggressive frames are made with a **universal frame system (USF)**, which means that the frames are made to fit all aggressive skates.*

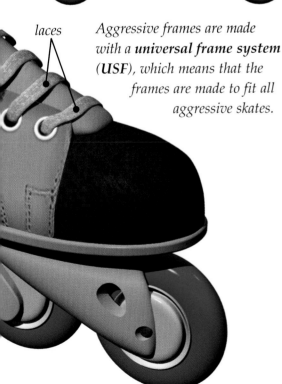

THE WHEEL THING

Most vert and street skaters use similar boots, but they customize the size and fitting of their wheels to fit their style. Larger wheels give a skater more speed, but smaller wheels are better for grinding. Most skaters use a **flat fitting**, which has all the wheels at the same level. Skates with a flat fitting are also known as **flat rockers**.

ROCK OUT

Some skaters prefer to have their wheels at different levels to allow for easier tricks or sharper turns. The **anti-rocker** skate has two middle wheels that are higher than the outer wheels. Anti-rocker skates are slow, but they are very easy to grind.

A DIFFERENT SKATE

There are a few differences between aggressive and recreational in-line skates. Aggressive skates have short frames and no heel brakes, whereas recreational skates have longer frames and a heel brake at the back of each frame. Long frames and brakes can get in the way during an aggressive skater's complex tricks. Their skates also have heels with extra cushioning to help make hard landings easier.

SKATEPARKS

Some cities don't allow aggressive in-line skating in the streets because skaters can cause damage to public property. **Skateparks** have become a street skater's paradise. They are full of pipe ramps and street obstacles on which skaters can perform tricks. Skateparks were invented in the 1970s for skateboarders. Today, aggressive skaters also use them.

Vert skaters build up speed on a half-pipe by **pumping***, or going from one side to the other.*

NOT YOUR GRANDPA'S PIPE

Pipe ramps are very large and are often made of strong, flexible plywood. The curved parts of the ramps are known as **transitions**. The top of the ramp is called the **lip**. The lip is covered by a metal tube known as the **coping**. There are two main types of pipe ramps. A **half-pipe** has two transitions that face one another. A **quarter-pipe** has only one transition.

POOL PARTY

In addition to pipe ramps, skateparks have **pools** and **bowls** for skaters to **carve** around. Pools are like swimming pools with the water drained out. Bowls are similar to pools, but they have a circular shape. Vert skaters ride up and down the steep walls of pools and bowls to build speed, just as they do on pipe ramps.

A LOT OF FUN

Many obstacles at skateparks—stairs, railings, and curbs—are just like those found on streets. **Fun boxes**, however, are obstacles found only at skateparks. A fun box combines several obstacles into one. It usually has raised edges like small ramps and railings or bars for grinding. Each fun box is a little different from the next.

rail

fun box

mini ramp

bowl

Mini ramps have small curved transitions. They launch a skater straight into the air.

13

GRIND IT DOWN

*A skater performs a **soul** grind by using the **sole**, or bottom, of the rear skate's boot to grind. If the skater uses the front skate's boot, it is called an **alley-oop soul**. These are two of the most common grinds.*

Performing grinds is an important part of aggressive skating, especially street skating. Grinds get their name from the sound the skates make as they slide along a railing, curb, bar, or other obstacle. These tricks require a lot of speed and incredible balance. **Bailing**, or falling, can be very painful!

GRIND POSITIONS

There are many types of grinds. Each one uses different skate and leg positions as the skater slides along the obstacle. The possibilities are endless! For example, a grind can be done with the bottom of the frame, the side of the frame, or the bottom of the boot. A skater can grind on one or both skates. Even the direction in which the feet are pointing can change with different grinds. Skaters are always making up new positions to create more difficult grinds.

DAILY GRINDS

Although there are too many grinds to name, here are a few favorites. Don't get tangled up!

X grind: *crossing the legs so the outside edges of each skate's boot and frame grind on opposite sides of the railing*

Makio grind: *grinding on one foot only*

Shifty: *grinding the inside edge of the front boot and the outside edge of the rear boot*

Backslide: *grinding on the back boot only*

Acid grind: *grinding so the back boot is pointing sideways while the front foot is pointing straight ahead*

Disaster: *grinding on an obstacle to which the skater has been launched from a great height*

TRICKY RIDING

Aggressive skaters have the freedom to ride almost anywhere. The best skaters are fearless, and many of their tricks are unusual. These athletes ride on walls and zoom down stairs without falling or slowing down. They'll even balance on balcony railings, if given the chance! These tricks show just how inventive skaters can be.

STALLING FOR TIME

A **stall** is similar to a grind, but rather than sliding, the skater must pause and balance on the obstacle. Railings, bars, curbs, or a ramp's coping are all great places for stalls. Once on the obstacle, the skater holds his or her position for a few seconds before coming down. Another stall, called the **invert**, is just like a handstand. To perform an invert, a skater turns upside down at the top of the ramp and balances on the coping with one hand. When stalls and grinds are performed on the lip of a ramp, they are also known as **lip tricks**.

*The longer a skater can hold an invert, the more impressive the trick is. Skaters can make an invert even more thrilling by performing a **grab** at the same time.*

Fly on the Wall

Street skaters can perform some amazing tricks—they can even ride on walls! **Wallrides** are done by leaping on a wall and riding along it. Skaters build up a lot of speed before jumping. The speed keeps skaters on the wall and off the ground.

Take the Stairs

Street skaters often have to skate up or down stairs when they are skating in the city. They put one foot just ahead of the other to keep their balance while going down the stairs. Skaters can go down stairs forward or backward.

TAKE FLIGHT

Aerial tricks, including grabs, **spins**, and **flips**, are among the most breathtaking in aggressive skating. Street skaters perform these tricks as they leap over obstacles such as stairs and benches. The greatest stage for aerials, however, is the pipe ramp used in vert. Vert skaters use pipe ramps to launch themselves more than ten feet (3 m) above the coping.

Some pros can perform a 1080 spin, which is three full rotations!

ROUND AND ROUND

Spins and flips are dazzling aerials. In a spin, the skater's body rotates in midair like a flying top. A spin gets its name from the number of degrees in the rotation. A half rotation is 180 degrees, so the spin is called a 180. A full rotation spin is called a 360. To do a flip, the skater turns head over heels. There are both front flips and back flips. A **brainless** is a back flip done while performing a 540 spin. The name refers to any skater who is crazy enough to try it!

MAKE A GRAB

The skater shown above is crossing a **gap**, or large space, while doing a mute grab. To do grab tricks, skaters grab parts of their skates with their hands while in midair. Like grinds, there are several types of grabs. Skaters can use many different leg positions or grab different parts of the skate. Here are a few cool grab tricks:

Method: *grabbing one skate with the same-side hand*
Mute: *reaching around the legs and grabbing at least one skate with the opposite hand*
Rocket: *grabbing the skates while both legs are extended in front of the skater*
Liu Kang: *grabbing one skate and kicking the other skate straight out to the side*

COMPETITIONS

Competitions offer skaters the chance to show off their talent and to see how they measure up to one another. The ASA organizes vert and street events around the world. It also keeps track of the rankings of the best skaters. The ASA even holds **amateur** events for talented skaters who aren't yet pros. The X Games and the Gravity Games are the biggest extreme-sports competitions. These events feature top aggressive in-line skaters as well as pro BMX riders and skateboarders. During a competition, the skaters usually have two **runs** that last a minute each. In that short time, a skater must perform as many impressive grinds, stalls, spins, and flips as he or she can. Judges evaluate the skater's style, smoothness, creativity, and the overall difficulty of the tricks.

ADD IT UP

A skater earns many points by performing difficult and creative tricks. The best way to make tricks more challenging is to use **combinations**. Combinations can be executed by performing two tricks at the same time. For example, a skater can make a 180 spin while doing a mute grab. Combinations can also be a few tricks strung together one after another. Grinding a bar and then jumping off and performing a grab is a popular combination.

MAKING MONEY

Pros may love skating, but they couldn't do it full time if they didn't get paid! Most competitions have cash prizes for the top skaters. Winning competitions helps in other ways, too. The best pros earn money through **endorsements**, or deals that pay them to use or advertise a company's products.

If a skater performs a 360, to an X grind, and then a method grab, the combination is listed like this— "360-X-method."

SKATING STARS

Aggressive skating is barely ten years old, but it already has its share of superstars. Some of the skaters on these pages are legends who helped build the sport's popularity. Others are current stars who are taking aggressive in-line to greater heights. When it comes to flying off ramps or grinding obstacles, these pros have no fear!

EITO AND TAKESHI YASUTOKO

These vert skating brothers from Osaka, Japan, come from a family of in-line skaters. Eito (shown above) is known for his fearless skating. He is one of very few skaters to perform a 1440 flat spin—that's four full midair rotations with the body in a horizontal position! Eito has won numerous events as well as a number-one world ranking for vert in 2001. His brother Takeshi is one of the youngest pros skating today. Takeshi won a medal at the X Games when he was only fifteen.

RANDY "ROADHOUSE" SPIZER

This pro started skating in Orange County, California, when he was only twelve. At the age of fifteen, Spizer won the first ASA street finals. Nearly ten years later, he remains one of the world's most original street skaters. He is famous for landing grinds in almost impossible areas. He also helped increase the popularity of tricks like the X grind.

Brian Shima

With a style all his own, Shima, a California native, has been winning street titles all over the world. He may be only 5'5" (168 cm), but his ability to land 540 aerials over giant distances can make him the biggest skater in the park. Shima's daring skating amazes even other top pros. He recently started his own skate wheel company, called 4x4.

Jaren Grob

Grob's nickname is "The Monster" because of his outrageously daring tricks. In 2001, he was the ASA's number-one street skater, but this Utah skater is equally skilled in both vert and street events. Grob specializes in crossing giant gaps and easily landing huge **900**s, spins that are two-and-a-half rotations.

Fabiola da Silva

Brazilian skater "Fabi" is one of the best vert skaters in the world. She is an amazing street skater as well. In 1999, she won both the women's vert and street events at the first Gravity Games in Rhode Island, USA. Even when the ASA cancelled the women's vert competitions, she continued competing by entering the men's vert events.

THE NEED FOR SPEED

Not all extreme skaters are interested in daring tricks and jumps. Speed in-line skaters just want to go fast! These athletes use custom skates and powerful striding techniques to move at breakneck speeds of over 50 miles (80 km) per hour. Speed skaters wear tight-fitting clothing to prevent **wind resistance**. A loose t-shirt or baggy shorts would flap in the wind and slow down the skater.

BUILT FOR SPEED

Speed skates have long frames, no brakes, and five large, hard wheels that allow them to go farther and faster. Speed-skate boots are made of lightweight materials such as leather. The boots are very low-cut compared to other in-line skates, allowing skaters to stride as quickly as possible.

DOUBLE TIME

In-line skaters move forward by pushing against the ground with one skate and then the other. Normally, they push off once before switching to the other skate. Speed skaters, however, use a technique called the **double push** when striding to increase speed. The skaters make a "checkmark" pattern with their skate. A skater starts with legs wide apart and moves one skate in toward his or her body for the first short push. He or she then pivots the ankle, making a long, hard push outward. Speed skaters push with their heels, which gives more power than pushing from the toes.

Swinging the arms gives a speed skater a burst of extra power.

FEELING A DRAFT

When skaters are going fast, air drags on their bodies. It slows them down and makes them tired. Racers avoid this problem by **drafting**, or skating directly behind the skater ahead. The lead skater blocks the wind, giving the drafting skater a clearer path. A **pack**, or group of speed skaters, is often seen drafting. Each skater places his or her hands on the next skater's back.

Speed skaters stay low to the ground by bending at the hips and knees. Staying low helps make the skater's strides longer and more powerful.

OFF TO THE RACES

Speed in-line skating is all about racing. Most in-line races take place on country and city roads, but some races are held indoors on smooth, oval tracks called **velodromes**. The most common distance races are in-line marathons. They test each competitor's **endurance**, or ability to skate for a long time. Other types of races include **sprints**, **downhill**, and **slalom**. Each type of race requires slightly different skating techniques. All speed skaters need physical strength and good training to win races, however.

SHORT AND SWEET
Sprints are short, quick races. Some are only 328 feet (100 m) long, but others are up to 3 miles (5 km). Sprinters try to take the lead right away because the races end quickly.

DOWN THEY GO
Downhill races are the fastest and most thrilling. Racers must be in perfect control at all times. At extremely high speeds, even the slightest mistake can result in a big wipeout!

WEAVING IN AND OUT

In slalom events, racers weave back and forth around small pylons. The pylons are usually placed in a straight line about five to six feet (1-2 m) apart. Slalom racers use recreational in-line skates because they turn more quickly than speed skates do. In speed slalom, racers try to get through the course with the fastest time. In figure slalom, skaters impress judges with tricks such as weaving through pylons on one skate.

GOING THE DISTANCE

Distance races are usually 26 miles (42 km) long, but they can be as long as 62 miles (100 km). The key to distance racing is staying with the leading pack of skaters. A skater too far behind the pack usually wastes energy catching up, and winning the race becomes impossible. The most famous distance race is the 86-mile (138 km) Athens-to-Atlanta, which takes place in Georgia every year.

Sprints are held on tracks such as velodromes, where short distances can be measured exactly.

SAFE SKATING

Safety equipment is important for all in-line skaters. Even pros have accidents! Protective gear and helmets keep skaters safe when they fall, so they can skate again another day. Helmets and gear should always be in good condition and fit properly. The equipment should be snug, but not too tight.

Aggressive in-line skaters can wear whatever they want, but the clothing should be comfortable. Speed skaters wear tight clothing.

helmet

elbow pads

glove

wrist pad

knee pads

Gloves are important to aggressive skaters. They allow skaters to perform inverts without scraping their palms.

Whereas some of the famous skaters in this book may not be wearing proper safety gear, a beginner should always put on a helmet and pads before skating!

Pads have a plastic shell that protects joints such as knees and elbows. Velcro straps keep the pads firmly in place during tricks.

An in-line helmet is made of light, hard foam that is covered by a tough plastic shell. The inside has a soft padded lining that cushions the head. The chin strap should always be snug, or the helmet will fall off.

WE ALL FALL DOWN

Not every bail has to be a painful one. Proper safety equipment allows skaters to bail without getting hurt. When bailing, skaters try to fall forward. Falling forward allows them to land on their knees and palms, which are protected by pads and gloves. Most vert skaters use the **knee-slide bail** to escape a failed trick. The skaters simply drop to their knees and slide down the ramp.

USING COMMON SENSE

Common sense is just as important as protective gear. When skating in public places, there are cars, pedestrians, and cyclists. Skaters need to be aware of the traffic around them. In a skatepark, skaters must be patient and wait their turns. If they don't, overcrowding on ramps and obstacles could lead to nasty collisions between skaters.

TAKE IT IN STRIDE

In-line skating is great exercise, and almost anyone can do it. With a pair of skates and the proper protective gear, you can have fun and stay in shape. Before you even think of trying extreme skating, however, you must master the basics. Aggressive in-line and speed skating require a lot of practice.

FINDING HELP

Finding a good instructor is an important first step. An instructor will teach you everything from proper skating techniques to the benefits of stretching and healthy eating. You will also learn how to skate safely and how to avoid injuries. Skate shops or fitness centers are good places to hook up with an instructor. The International Inline Skating Association (IISA) also has a website that helps beginner skaters locate instructors.

WHAT TO BUY

When buying your first pair of skates, check your local skate or sports shop. Ask for basic in-line skates, complete with a heel brake and large wheels. You can upgrade to aggressive skates later, when you are a stronger skater. Try on different skates and see what feels most comfortable. Remember, you should be most concerned with the skate's comfort and fit.

GET THE LATEST

If you are looking for some inspiration, in-line skating is everywhere! Many in-line magazines, such as *Daily Bread*, showcase top pros, new equipment, the latest tricks, and great photos. Sports channels also run programs on extreme sports events featuring aggressive in-line skating. One of the easiest places to learn more is on the Internet. Here are a few websites to get you started:

www.inlineskating.about.com - this is a great place to learn about the terms, styles, and history of in-line
www.iisa.org - the official site of the International Inline Skating Association
http://www.asaskate.com - the ASA's official site, where you can catch up on all the latest news on the pro tour

GLOSSARY

Note: Boldfaced words that are defined in the book may not appear in the glossary.

amateur Describing a person who loves to skate but does not earn a living doing it

bearings Parts of a skate wheel that allow the wheel to rotate smoothly

carve To skate around the walls inside a bowl

frame A hard plastic bar on the bottom of an in-line skate boot into which the wheels are set

grab A trick done when a skater grabs part of a skate with his or her hand while in midair

professional An expert in-line skater who earns a living by competing in the sport

roller rink A building containing a flat area used for roller skating or in-line skating

run The routine a skater performs during a competition

pipe ramp A giant ramp with curved sloping sides used in vert skating

recreational Non-aggressive in-line skating which is performed for fitness or fun

skatepark An indoor or outdoor park full of obstacles on which skaters can practice

toe brake A brake found at the front end of an in-line skate

wind resistance The slowing down that occurs when a skater rides against the wind during a race

X Games A series of extreme sports competitions

INDEX

1 2 3 4 5 6 7 8 9 0   Printed in the U.S.A.   3 2 1 0 9 8 7 6 5 4